Looking After Your
· HORSE ·
& PONY

Looking After Your
· HORSE ·
& PONY

· Edited by Ian Kearey ·

PARRAGON

First published in Great Britain in 1997 by
Parragon
Unit 13–17
Avonbridge Trading Estate
Atlantic Road
Avonmouth
Bristol BS11 9QD

ISBN: 0-7525-2159-4

Produced by Haldane Mason, London.

Acknowledgements
Art Director: **Ron Samuels**
Design: **Digital Artworks Partnership Ltd**
Illustration: **Robert Farnworth**
Picture Research: **Charles Dixon-Spain**

Printed in Italy

Picture Acknowledgements
All photographs by **Only Horses**

Material in this book has previously appeared in
The Complete Book of Horse & Pony Care
by Mike Janson and Juliana Kembell-Williams

· CONTENTS ·

Markings

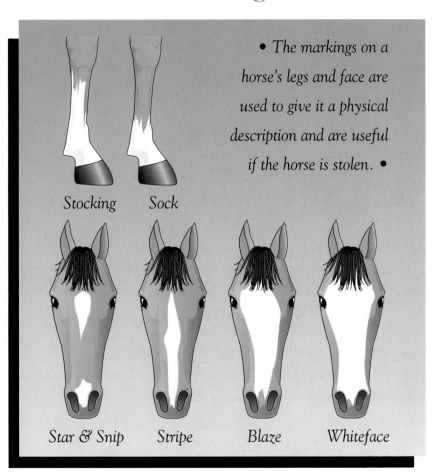

• *The markings on a horse's legs and face are used to give it a physical description and are useful if the horse is stolen.* •

Stocking   Sock

Star & Snip   Stripe   Blaze   Whiteface

Foot or hoof

• Hooves should be cool to the touch, the frog free from cracks and the horn hard and smooth. •

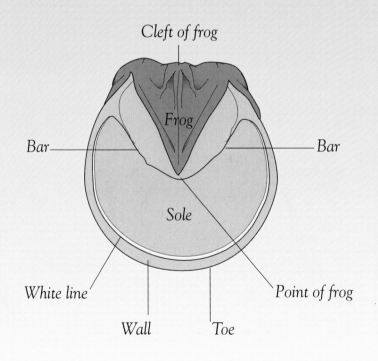

Cleft of frog

Frog

Bar — — Bar

Sole

White line

Point of frog

Wall   Toe

General points

• The horse's head should be in good proportion to the body, the eyes large and set well apart and the ears set towards the front of the head. The neck should be curved and crested at the top and the back relatively straight, with only a slight dip between the top of the rump and the withers. •

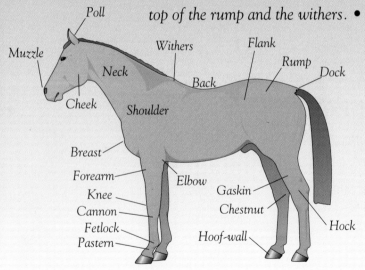

Poll

Muzzle

Withers

Flank

Rump

Dock

Neck

Back

Cheek

Shoulder

Breast

Forearm

Elbow

Gaskin

Knee

Chestnut

Cannon

Fetlock

Hock

Pastern

Hoof-wall

Making a choice

Once you have found a potentially suitable horse, it is time to take a closer look at it.

Take an experienced person with you, because no amount of reading will substitute for practical experience. Equally important, go with an open mind and be prepared to refuse.

It is easy to become carried away with the excitement of having your own horse or pony, and want to buy the first one you see. The more animals you see, the better the chance of making the right match, and the more you will learn.

When assessing a horse you are checking for three things – its temperament and social manners, its overall health and fitness and what is known as its conformation. Basically, conformation is the term for a horse's physical characteristics and the proportions of its body, legs, neck and head in relationship to each other. Obviously this will vary between different breeds, but there are a few basics which can affect the way a horse moves and performs, as well as its overall attractiveness.

HORSE COSTS

The cost of a horse has many components beyond the initial purchase price. Some can be planned for and some not, and there are many 'hidden extras'. The following is a general guide to the range of costs one might plan for, with notations of some of the additions you may find essential.

- Basic subsistence: livery, field rent, feed and bedding
- Basic tack: saddle, bridle, headcollar, lead rope, tack rack
- Additional tack: martingale, special bits, lunging rope
- Horse and protective clothing: winter rug, sweat rug, bandages, working boots
- Grooming equipment: curry comb, brushes, hoof pick
- Cleaning equipment: saddle soap, sponges
- Health products: liniment, sprays, hoof oil, etc.
- Clothing for everyday riding: hat, trousers, boots
- Clothing for showing/hunting/eventing: jacket, boots, jodphurs/britches, shirt, ties, stock and stock-pins, gloves, back-protector
- Showing costs
- Veterinary charges
- Insurance

Owning a horse

Owning your own horse allows you to ride whenever you want, rather than having to book designated hours at a riding or livery stable.

But, more importantly, it allows you to develop a riding relationship with one horse so that together you can learn and improve.

Horse and rider will begin to understand one another's temperament and moods, and if the rider is consistent with his or her signals the horse will learn how to respond.

A horse that is ridden each week by several different people – in all probability of differing height, weight and riding ability – cannot be expected to be consistent in its performance. And having your own horse, like any other animal, teaches you the need for responsibility and compassion.

Horses take time, money and an investment in care that far exceeds that necessary for any other pet. It is essential to be honest as to how much time you can commit and how much you can afford, because the horse will need both in varying amounts, depending on the breed of horse, how it is kept and for what purpose it is used.

Chapter 1

A New Horse

*O*nce you have become certain that horse-riding is the sport or hobby that you wish to pursue, then you will probably take the next step and consider buying your own horse or pony.

There are several advantages to owning your own horse and several disadvantages – all of which should be weighed carefully before you make your decision.

The purchase of a horse or pony is a serious commitment which can give years of pleasure or could just as easily be a disappointing experience.

A well-trained young foal will provide many years of pleasure.

Before making a decision, it is worth considering how much time you will be able to spend on training your horse or pony – if this is likely to be limited, a horse that is already trained may be the answer.

In addition, be prepared to talk to people who work full-time with horses – owners, grooms and even veterinarians – although they are bound to have differing ideas, you will gather valuable information to help you make a choice.

• *Girl and pony – best of friends.*

Introduction

Horses and humans have lived and worked together for more than 5,000 years, with the horse providing transport and being the prime draught animal, warhorse and sporting companion. Today, the horse is mostly used for sport and recreation. More people are riding now than ever before – the horse has retained its magic, and is as popular as ever. Horses are versatile creatures and have something to offer to everybody, from racing to showing, leisure riding to eventing, show-jumping to playing polo.

What you choose to do is up to you, but how you choose what to do is the same – the relationship between the horse and rider is the most important thing. Experience breeds confidence in both horse and rider, and that only comes with spending time together. No two horses are alike, and only you can gather the practical experience, make the correct decisions and learn from your own mistakes. For some people, horses become a time-consuming passion for life, but if any animal deserves it, it is the horse.

Training the rider

A good rider needs to be fit, with good muscle tone in the legs, stomach and back.

While a certain amount of physical strength is called for, good muscle control and responsiveness over the whole body are more important than strong arms. Riding can be tiring, and the fitter you are, the more likely you are to be able to enjoy it.

Flexibility is important, as a good rider needs to be able to move and change position quickly and easily. Good balance is an essential. The nature of a horse's movements require you constantly to change your centre of gravity. You need to be able to do this instinctively so that you can concentrate on direction and control.

Perhaps the most important ingredient to achieving a good standard of riding ability is attitude. To be a good rider you have to want to ride and to have a fondness, if not outright love, for horses.

Horses are very instinctive animals and will respond quickly to signs of tension or fear in their riders. Riding is not a matter of rider dominating horse – it is a partnership between both.

Chapter 2

Training and Tack

*R*egular training for both horse and rider will increase your enjoyment of riding. By training together, you learn together and create that special bond that will allow you to develop your confidence and competence.

It is not necessary to achieve a high standard of competence to be able to enjoy the pleasure of sitting astride a horse, but if you do hope to become an accomplished rider, it is as important to train yourself as it is to train your mount.

A good rider can make up for many faults in a horse's training, but a well-trained horse can never compensate for a poor rider.

It is essential that you have the right tack to fit your horse, that you know how to fit it, and, as it is expensive, how to look after it properly.

Generally, the less tack you have to use at one time, the better the riding experience for both yourself and your mount.

At full speed.

• *Mother and daughter turned out for a show.*

• *Lunging in a paddock: the rope, or lunge, is controlled by the helper, while the rider works with the horse to build up its ability to understand commands and respond to them appropriately and immediately. This is no substitute for hard work and patience when training a horse or pony, but perseverence will pay dividends; the result will be a well-tempered, supple and responsive mount that is a joy to ride.*

Riding positions

The ability to ride begins with your position in the saddle, commonly referred to as one's seat.

A good seat is one where you have maximum body contact with the saddle, which allows you to remain as close as possible to the horse, and the correct positioning of back, arms and legs to maintain balance. A good seat encourages a relaxed body in control of itself.

The basics of a good seat are first, to position yourself squarely in the middle of the saddle between pommel and cantle. Second, straighten your back and head so that that they are comfortably aligned, shoulders back and your eyes looking between the horse's ears. Third, relax your shoulders and let your arms between shoulder and elbow hang naturally at your sides. Fourth, position your hands either side of the horse's neck so that your forearms are angled slightly inwards. The hands should always be kept low.

The position of the legs is perhaps most important, as it is these which anchor you to your mount and give you the most body contact with the horse.

• *Sitting quietly before moving off prepares both rider and horse for the tasks ahead. It also gives the rider time to settle into his or her riding position.*

Mounting

The process of mounting is a good test of both a rider's flexibility and a horse's manners. Not all horses enjoy the shift of weight involved in mounting, and it is not uncommon for them to refuse to stand still. It is therefore important that a rider mounts as quickly and smoothly as possible.

Always mount from the horse's near, or left, side. Take the reins evenly in your left hand so that you have light contact with his mouth, and grasp the pommel of the saddle. Facing towards the horse's tail, take the stirrup iron in your right hand and turn it clockwise towards you so it is parallel to the horse's body. Insert your left foot. Using your left foot as a pivot point, pull your body up, swing your right leg over the horse's rump and down the other side, while maintaining your balance over the middle of the horse with the left hand. Find your right stirrup with your right foot, avoiding poking the horse with your toe, and slide your foot in.

Basic gaits

All horses have four basic gaits – walk, trot, canter and gallop.

For each of these the rider needs to adopt a slightly different position on the horse in terms of weight distribution, legs, seat and hands. To move between these gaits, the horse will expect certain cues which the rider must learn.

Walking is the slowest of a horse's gaits but nevertheless provides the ideal opportunity for horse and rider to 'get the feel' of one another.

The trot is a bouncy two-beat pace which, depending on the individual horse, can be very jarring. Most riders rise in the saddle to the trot, which is known as posting or rising trot.

The canter is probably the most enjoyable gait. It consists of a three-beat rolling motion to which the rider generally sits.

The gallop is the final and fastest gait, consisting of a rapid four-time step sequence. Galloping for a beginner would be inadvisable, because, apart from being fast and therefore dangerous, a good deal of balance is required on the rider's part.

Training the horse

All horses require different amounts and kinds of training.

During the course of its life, a horse will usually have had several different owners – each with his own style of riding, level of experience and approach to keeping and caring for it. A horse may also have been used for many different purposes.

At its most basic, training is a matter of ensuring that a horse is fit, well-mannered, understands its cues and is reliable. Some types of training, such as breaking-in a young horse or preparing a horse for eventing, are highly specialized and require professional help.

Written guides such as this are no substitute for years of experience.

Most training, however, is actually done at a day-to-day level. Every time you ride your horse it gains more experience – of you and of its surroundings. The important thing to remember is that a horse is capable of learning bad habits as well as good, and to prevent it from learning these is as important a form of training as any other.

• *Pony and rider learning together.*

Good manners

Whatever the standard or ability of a horse, above all else it should be trained to observe good manners both in the stable and when riding out.

At walk, the horse should keep a steady pace, not slowing down or speeding up suddenly. At trot, the horse should maintain an even rhythm without the need for undue pressure on the bit.

When cantering, the horse should remain collected and not pull on the bit or attempt to race.

The ability to halt, stand still, and back on command is a sign of a well-schooled horse. This indicates not only that the horse is sensitive to the bit but also that he is attentive to the rider and under control. Many horses find it difficult to stand still, particularly when asked to come to a halt from a fast trot or canter. This is partly a matter of practice so the horse understands what is expected of him, but may also call for calming tactics such as shifting weight to the back of the saddle, a soothing voice and a reassuring pat.

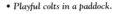

• *Playful colts in a paddock.*

Saddles

When choosing a saddle, it should fit both horse and rider.

For the horse's comfort, the saddle must be wide enough to avoid pinching the spine and below the withers, and high enough to clear the withers by about 5 cm (2 in), or allow you to put three fingers between the withers and the pommel.

The rider should be able to sit in the middle of the saddle without touching either the pommel or cantle, and it must be of the correct width, so that the rider's leg muscles are not stretched. Saddles are made in a standard selection of widths and lengths, and it is a question of selecting the correct combination.

There are basically three types of saddle – the general riding saddle, dressage and show-jumping. There are, however, only minor variations between them which mainly affect the height of the pommel and cantle, and the cut and angle of the flap. The leather covering can be any colour, and can be plain or decoratively tooled. Saddles also have knee-rolls which support the knees and thighs of the rider.

Saddles

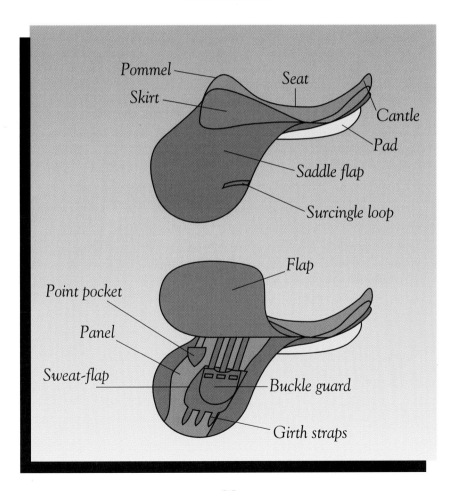

Pommel

Skirt

Seat

Cantle

Pad

Saddle flap

Surcingle loop

Flap

Point pocket

Panel

Sweat-flap

Buckle guard

Girth straps

Girths and stirrups

**The saddle is held in place by a girth which buckles
on to straps under the main saddle flap and which can be
adjusted for length.**

The most common type is an even strip about 8 cm (3 in) wide, made of
fabric or woven nylon, which is less likely to stretch in wet weather than
traditional leather.

The stirrup irons are attached by stirrup leathers to the saddle, and these
in turn are hooked on to a metal clip at the top of the skirt and adjusted
for length by a buckle. The clips are designed as a safety
feature, so if a rider falls and his foot gets stuck in the
stirrup iron, the leather will slip off to prevent the
rider from being dragged along. Some saddles have a
surcingle loop to hold the extra length of
the leathers.

The most usual stirrup iron is called the plain iron, which
can be fitted with a rubber pad to prevent the foot from
slipping. Always choose an iron big enough to ensure that
your foot cannot become jammed in it if you fall.

Bits

• *The metal bit which is fitted into the horse's mouth is one of the means by which the rider controls the horse, changes direction and stops. There are various designs, which exercise differing amounts of control. All bits are designed to put pressure on a part of the horse's head and/or mouth.* •

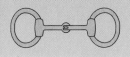

Snaffle: upwards on the corners of the mouth.

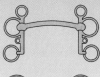

Pelham: upwards on the corners of the mouth, downwards on the tongue bars, curb groove and poll.

Double bridle: upwards on the corners of the mouth, downwards on the bars, curb groove and poll.

Martingales

A martingale is used on horses that have a tendency to carry their heads too high, in an attempt to avoid the bit and lessen a rider's control.

There are two commonly used kinds. The standing martingale is attached to the underside of a cavesson noseband and the girth, with a neck strap to hold it in place. This puts pressure on the horse's nose if it throws its head up. When positioned correctly, the standing martingale should form a straight line between the girth and noseband when the horse's head is held at the right height.

The running martingale has two straps that run from the girth to the reins and are then threaded through the rings. When the horse's head and the rider's hands are in the right position, the martingale should be adjusted so that the reins run in a straight line from hands to bit. The running martingale pulls on the horse's mouth if it lifts its head.

Bridles

• Bridles only vary in size to make a good fit on the horse's head. The headpiece sits behind the horse's ears and is buckled to the cheekpieces which run alongside the horse's cheeks and are attached to the bit rings. The browband is set in front of the horse's ears. •

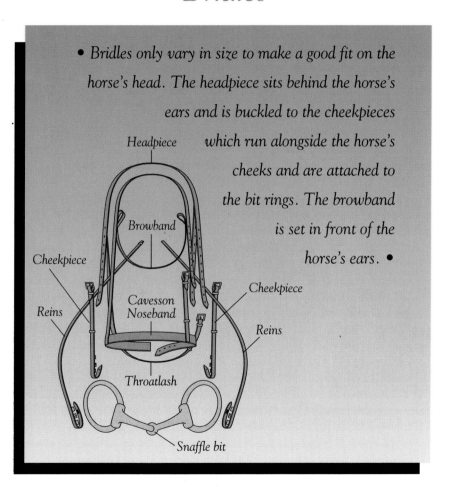

Headpiece

Browband

Cheekpiece

Reins

Cavesson
Noseband

Cheekpiece

Reins

Throatlash

Snaffle bit

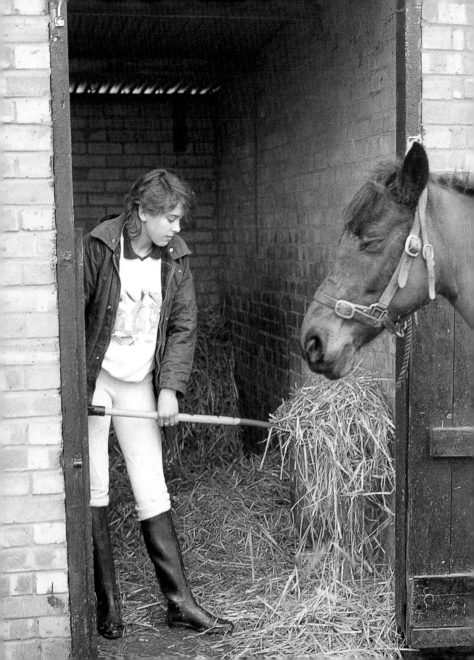

Chapter 3

Feeding and Caring for Your Horse

*C*aring for your horse is more than simply riding it, although naturally regular exercise is important to keep it fit.

Looking after a horse means, among other things, providing food and shelter, grooming, shoeing and general health care. While some horses seem to fend for themselves, others – especially if they have Arab or Thoroughbred blood – need a lot more attention.

Horses need food for the same reason as humans: general health, growth and energy to work.

A young, growing horse, or one that is exercised and worked hard, has a greater requirement of energy than one that is turned out to graze most of the time.

A contented pony grazing at the end of the day.

• *Mucking out is part of the stable routine.*

Feeding

A horse that does little work can be turned out and left to feed on good grass in summer and be given hay and high-protein feed supplements in winter.

A pony or small horse will need at least 0.5 hectares (1 acre) of good grass, and preferably more, to have enough natural food without the need for supplementary feeding. A stabled horse will need to be fed every day with a balance of bulk fibre food, such as hay, and supplementary food that provides adequate levels of protein, fats, carbohydrates, vitamins and minerals.

Bulk foods are grass, hay, carrots and bran, while concentrate foods such as barley, maize and oats are high in fats and carbohydrates. Both kinds provide varying amounts of protein, vitamins and salts. Proprietary, ready-mixed horse food, available from feed merchants, has a balanced ration which saves owners from mixing up the ingredients themselves.

Water

A horse will drink up to 45 litres (10 gallons) of water a day, and half as much again in hot weather.

It is essential that a horse, whether turned out or stabled, has access to an unlimited supply of water. Buckets are not always practical, as a horse will drink a bucketful in one go, and they are all too easily knocked over. Unless you are lucky enough to have a stream with easy access for the horse, the best solution is a trough that is connected to the mains supply and fed by an automatic valve.

The alternative is to keep it topped up regularly by hose or bucket. In the stable, a drinking bowl should be provided, ideally one that self-fills.

In winter, when there are heavy frosts, the water trough should be checked daily to make sure that it has not frozen over. An old tennis ball left to float on the surface will keep it clear to a certain extent, otherwise the ice will have to be broken up.

Turned-out horses

Whether turned out permanently or for part of the day, a horse will need some kind of shelter to protect it from wind and rain all year round, and the attention of insects in summer.

A field shelter should be large enough for several horses and have one open side facing north, so that it does not receive sun. A hay-rack, or rings for attaching hay-nets, should be fitted on the inside so that the horse can be fed in the dry in winter. A salt lick kept inside will also help to discourage the horse from chewing trees and fencing if it is short of minerals.

When a horse is turned out, it is relatively self-sufficient in food and water, but this does not mean that it can look after itself entirely. The horse should be visited every day to have its feet picked out and be checked over for knocks and scratches. Another regular task is worming every six or eight weeks, especially if the field is small and the danger of parasites consequently greater.

• *Enjoying the freedom of a paddock.*

Stabled horses

The stabled horse needs to be looked after every day, and a basic stable routine takes up an enormous amount of time and can never be missed.

It begins early in the morning and finishes in early evening. The first thing to do in the morning is to check the horse for any damage or injuries that it may have inflicted on itself during the night, and to adjust the night blanket if it has slipped. The horse will then need to be fed and the drinking water replaced.

Stabled horses need regular exercise to keep them fit, stop them becoming bored and difficult, and to ensure that they give a good ride. There is no fixed exercise routine, as it will depend on the breed and size of the horse and the kind of work it will be expected to do.

A hunter, for example, needs more exercise than a native pony. One basic rule is never to exercise a horse until an hour and a half after a heavy feed, and to keep the hay-net away for at least an hour beforehand.

• *A riding school outing.*

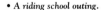

Shoeing

The horse's feet should be checked at least every six weeks, and preferably every four.

The horn of a horse's hoof is continually growing from the top of the hoof, producing about 2.5 cm (1 in) each month. A horse out at grass may be able to manage without shoes, as the horn is worn down at the same rate as it grows, but any horse worked on hard surfaces will need to be shod, otherwise the horn will be worn away, leading to lameness.

Whether shod or not, the hooves will need to be trimmed regularly, to prevent the hoof wall cracking and splitting. Equally, uneven wear due to the horse's conformation needs to be corrected, otherwise the conformation problems place undue strain on the tendons. Trimming also maintains the correct alignment of the hoof and pastern. Although the toe horn grows faster than the heel, a horse at grass is likely to wear down the toes more quickly, and the heel will need to be trimmed. A shod horse tends to wear the heel horn as there is more friction when it moves, so the toes will need to be trimmed more often.

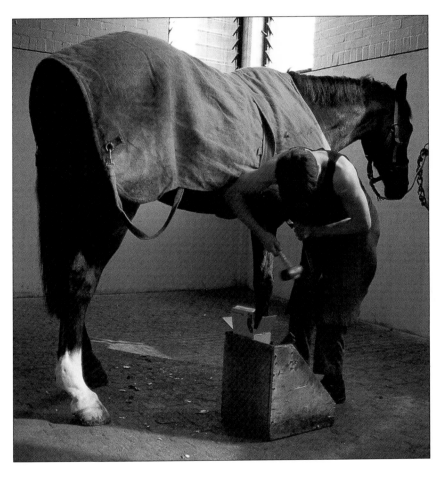

• *Most horses become used to regular visits from the farrier, and can be shod relatively quickly.*

Grooming

Grooming is more than a way of making a horse look attractive – it also helps to keep the horse healthy, tones up muscle, and improves circulation and the condition of its coat.

Most horses also enjoy the attention. Stabled horses will need to be groomed every day before exercise. A light groom, known as quartering, removes dirt and dust with a body brush, concentrating on the areas that are underneath the saddle, girth and bridle.

Turned-out horses need less grooming than stabled horses, as they need a certain amount of grease in their coat to keep them warm and repel moisture. Vigorous brushing will remove the natural grease. They will, however, need to have their winter coat brushed out with a curry comb as the weather warms up.

Grass-kept horses tend to roll a lot, covering themselves with mud. In itself, dried mud does no harm at all, but if it becomes wet again it irritates the skin and can lead to skin infections. Continual washing of the horse will strip out the natural water-repellent grease, so it is best to brush out the mud when it is dry.

GROOMING KIT

All grooming kit should be kept tidy in a specially designed box or wire basket. Labelling each item with the name of either yourself or your horse helps to prevent losing things. Each horse should have its own grooming kit so that infections are not passed between different animals.

- Dandy brush: removes dried mud and sweat
- Body brush: removes dust and scurf
- Water brush: used on mane, tail and hooves
- Rubber curry comb: removes mud and dried sweat, and can be used as the metal curry comb
- Metal curry comb: used to clean the body brush, but never the horse
- Mane comb: used when trimming or plaiting mane or tail
- Sweat scraper sponges: removes sweat and water one is used on the eyes, nostrils and lips, the other on the dock
- Stable rubber: for the final polish of the coat
- Hoof oil and brush: shines up the hooves and prevents cracking
- Hoof pick: removes dirt and other objects from hoof

Clipping

If a horse is expected to work hard during winter, then clipping of the winter coat prevents it overheating.

There are different kinds of clip, depending on the amount of work the horse will do. None, however, should be done until the winter coat has fully grown in autumn and again in the New Year.

If the horse is clipped, it will need to wear a rug in the stable or a New Zealand rug if it is turned out during the day. Grass-kept horses should not be clipped.

The full clip is reserved for horses that undertake strenuous exercise, such as racehorses, but the most usual is the trace clip. The trace clip entails removing the coat from the underside of the neck, the stomach, the chest, and the fore and hind thighs. Hair is left on the legs.

The blanket clip removes the hair from the head and neck, but leaves hair on the legs and across the back where a blanket would lie. The hunter clip leaves hair on the legs and a saddle-shaped patch on the back and flanks.

Hunter clip

- This clip is reserved for horses which event, hunt or race during the winter. Do not use this clip if you are not going to compete or hunt. If you do use a hunter clip, make sure your horse or pony is blanketed at all times, whether stabled or turned out during the day. •

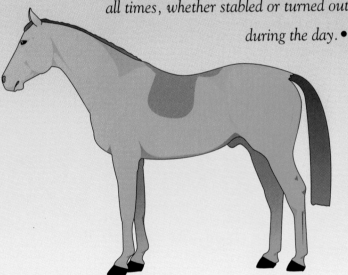

Trace High Clip

• A trace high clip is useful for horses and ponies kept at grass, as it affords them some protection while reducing sweating during exercise. Hair is removed from the belly up to the traces and halfway down the forearms and thighs. Hair beneath the neck can also be removed. •

Manes and tails

A horse's tail is designed so that it can keep its hindquarters free from flies and other biting insects, and should be kept long.

It can, however, be tidied by trimming it level with the hock.

If the hairs thicken around the root of the tail and become regularly soiled, these can be plucked out singly or in twos or threes by wrapping them around a tail comb and pulling sharply.

Bandaging also helps to tidy a tail, but make sure you dampen the tail before you start, as this makes the bandaging process easier. Do not, however, leave the tail bandage on overnight.

A thick, untidy mane that does not lie flat can also be plucked or pulled by removing the longest hairs from underneath. An evenly-pulled mane also helps to ensure that plaits are even.

Tail bandaging

• Tail bandaging keeps the top of the tail looking neat before showing, and protects it from rubbing when travelling in a box. •

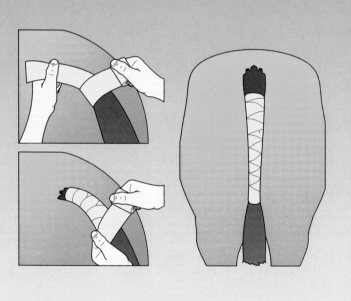

Mane plaiting

• *Divide the mane up into even bunches and hold each bunch together with an elastic band. Beginning at the poll, take off the elastic band from the first bunch of mane hair and dampen and then comb it straight. Plait tightly from the top to the end and sew up the end with plaiting thread. Wrap the thread around the spiky end*

and sew it under. Finally, roll the plait under to the neck and sew it in. Repeat the plaiting down the mane, making sure that the plaits are even. •

Chapter 4

Health Care

*A*s an owner, your responsibility is to recognize the signs of illness as early as possible and take the necessary action.

For the inexperienced owner, the rule should always be to call your veterinarian if you think there is a problem. It does help, however, if you learn to recognize and describe the symptoms to the veterinarian, as it will help the diagnosis. After all, you know your horse best.

A Lippizzaner stallion in the prime of health enjoying the mountain air in his Alpine paddock.

To recognize when a horse is unwell, it is important to know the signs of a healthy horse. A healthy horse is bright-eyed, has a shine to its coat, stands equally on all four feet and is alert and its ears should be warm to the touch at their base.

A healthy horse is interested in what is going on around it. A horse that becomes listless, stands in one place for a long time or is reluctant to move, is most probably sickening. Any change in normal behaviour or feeding routine suggests that there may be a problem.

• *The turned-out horse is often the healthiest.*

Preventative measures

All horses should be immunized against tetanus and influenza – and receive regular booster shots. They must also be wormed every four or six weeks.

All horses suffer from worms, which are parasites that live in the horse's intestines, feeding on the horse's digestive juices. Some also irritate the intestinal lining, making it harder for the horse to absorb nutrients. Many worm species invade the blood vessels and migrate to other organs, causing severe and permanent damage.

The horse becomes infected by eating worm larvae in field grass, which then enter the intestines where they develop into egg-laying adults. The eggs are discharged in the horse's droppings, and the breeding cycle starts again. Consequently, horses tend to have more worms in summer when they are grazing more, and will need to be wormed more regularly. If the field is used by several horses they should all be wormed at the same time. Good stable routine and good field management should help to cut down contamination.

Signs of worm infestation include a general poor condition with a dull coat, an extended stomach, anaemia, colic and an overall lack of performance.

FIRST-AID KIT

*All owners should have a first-aid kit stocked with every-
day medicines – kept close at hand in the tack room and
taken to any show or event. The kit should be regularly
checked, and any items used replaced immediately.
Make sure you also have a rudimentary knowledge of first-
aid for both horses and riders. Whilst it is useful to carry
first-aid kits around with you, there might be times when
you will have to resort to using whatever you can find
around you.*

The basic travelling kit for dealing with emergencies should contain:

- Gauze and crepe bandages
- Rolls of sticking plaster
- Cotton wool
- Gamgee
- Packet of lint
- Paraffin gauze dressing
- Bottle of antiseptic disinfectant
- Antibiotic aerosol spray and powder puffer
- Thermometer
- Surgical scissors (with rounded ends)

Skin problems

Horses are quite susceptible to skin problems, so good stable and field management are essential.

Ringworm is a fungal infection that is contagious. It is caught from other horses, and sometimes cattle, and it can be passed on to humans.

Sweet itch affects the area around the tail and mane, and causes the horse to rub these areas to ease the irritation. It is an allergic reaction to the bites of certain midges, which tend to attack the horse at dusk during late spring, summer and early autumn.

Lice are often found on horses in winter and spring, and can be passed on during grooming. They appear as small grey, black or yellow parasites in the coat which irritate the skin, making the horse scratch itself constantly, causing bald patches.

Warble-fly larvae can sometimes attack horses that graze with other animals, especially cattle.

Horses often develop lumps on their skin, which, if left, can turn to ulcerated sores. A common cause is badly fitting and dirty tack which rubs the horse's skin and leads to infection.

Teeth

• *Problems with teeth can make the horse stop eating properly, because chewing can be painful if teeth are sharp and overgrown. The teeth in opposite jaws wear each other down, ideally at a constant rate to keep the teeth balanced. In reality, they often wear unevenly, and the sharp edges of the teeth can cut the horse's mouth and tongue. Teeth should be checked regularly, and sharp edges should be rasped smooth by the veterinarian.* •

For rasping, the horse is controlled by a switch, bridle and halter.

Pulse, breathing and temperature

It is a good idea to know the normal pulse, breathing rate and temperature of your horse so that you can tell if it is feeling unwell or in pain. An individual horse's vital signs do vary, but whether at rest or recovering after heavy work, you will find these will usually remain within certain limits.

A normal pulse rate is somewhere between 35 and 40 per minute, but can be more than double this after being worked. The pulse can be found along the inside of the lower jaw or just behind the elbow.

A horse's normal breathing rate can vary from about 8 to 16 breaths a minute, with ponies tending to breathe faster than horses. Anything above this suggests that the horse is distressed and will probably have a temperature as well.

Take the temperature of your horse when he is fit and healthy and before exercise, and not when he is excited. It should read somewhere between 37.4°C (99.3°F) and 38.6°C (101.5°F) – anything higher suggests that the horse has a fever.

• *Ponies and riders going flat-out over a fence.*

Feet and legs

The most vulnerable part of a horse are its legs and feet, as the legs have to take knocks and carry the entire weight of the horse, and can twist on rough ground if the horse stumbles or falls.

The legs take a continual pounding, particularly on hard ground, and the feet can be damaged by poor shoeing, stray stones, sharp objects, and are highly susceptible to wet conditions, fever and inflammation.

Any damage to the horse's limbs must be taken seriously, and any sign of lameness examined by a veterinarian and diagnosed.

Lameness can be checked by asking someone to lead the horse at a slow trot to see if it favours a particular leg. Look out for the way it shifts its weight. Turning the horse usually makes the symptoms more marked. If a foreleg is giving problems, the horse will drop its head as the other one touches the ground.

Watch if he places his weight more on one hind leg than the other. When you have identified which leg is the problem, treatment is best left to the experts – veterinarian, farrier or blacksmith.

Seats of lameness

• *Lameness is the most common horse complaint and usually needs expert treatment. Check the lame leg for heat, pain and swelling, to find the site of the problem. Ninety per cent of lameness comes from problems with the foot.* •

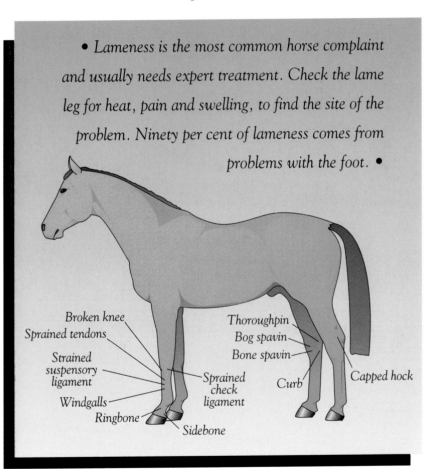

Broken knee
Sprained tendons
Strained suspensory ligament
Windgalls
Ringbone
Sidebone
Sprained check ligament
Thoroughpin
Bog spavin
Bone spavin
Curb
Capped hock

Colic

Colic is a severe digestive complaint which causes painful stomach-ache.

It should always be regarded as an emergency, and the veterinarian should be called immediately to give pain-killing injections and other treatment.

A horse suffering from colic will keep looking at its flanks, pawing the ground and begin sweating. It may start to roll on the ground, which presents the danger of a twisted intestine – and this can be fatal.

While waiting for the veterinarian, keep the horse on its feet, walk it around and cover it with a sweat rug or blanket to keep it warm.

The causes of colic are varied, and include poor or irregular feeding, too much water or exercise directly after a feed, and worm infections.

Index

Page numbers in *italic* refer to illustrations